Sunny Day Publishing, LLC
Cuyahoga Falls, Ohio 44223
www.sunnydaypublishing.com

A Walk With Dinosaurs
Copyright © 2020 Amber Justice
All rights reserved.

No part of this book may be used
or reproduced in any manner whatsoever
without written permission except
in the case of brief quotations embodied
in critical articles and reviews.

ISBN 978-1-948613-07-1

Printed in the United States of America

My Dad, Chuck, for being my biggest fan
and ever pushing me to reach higher.

My girls, Delayna and Savanna,
for their unwavering faith in my abilities.

My sister heart, Joanna, for being whatever I need
when I need it; Confidant, cheerleader, stress manager,
the one who always answers my calls.

My niece, Marley, the best 'Jr' editor you could ask for.

My husband, my best friend, the love of my life, Tim.

Lastly, but in no way the least, my son, Damien,
whom without his dinosaur obsession this book
would never have happened.

Thank you.

Spinosaurus was one of the
largest meat-eating dinosaurs.
That makes him a carnivore.
His name means 'Spine Lizard',
because of the large spines on his back.

Brachiosauruses were 40-foot herbivores.
They could weigh as much as
9 male elephants.
They were one of the largest, heaviest,
and tallest of the dinosaurs.

Ornithomimus could run as fast
As an ostrich, maybe more.
Its name means 'Bird Mimic'.
Like some birds, it was an omnivore.

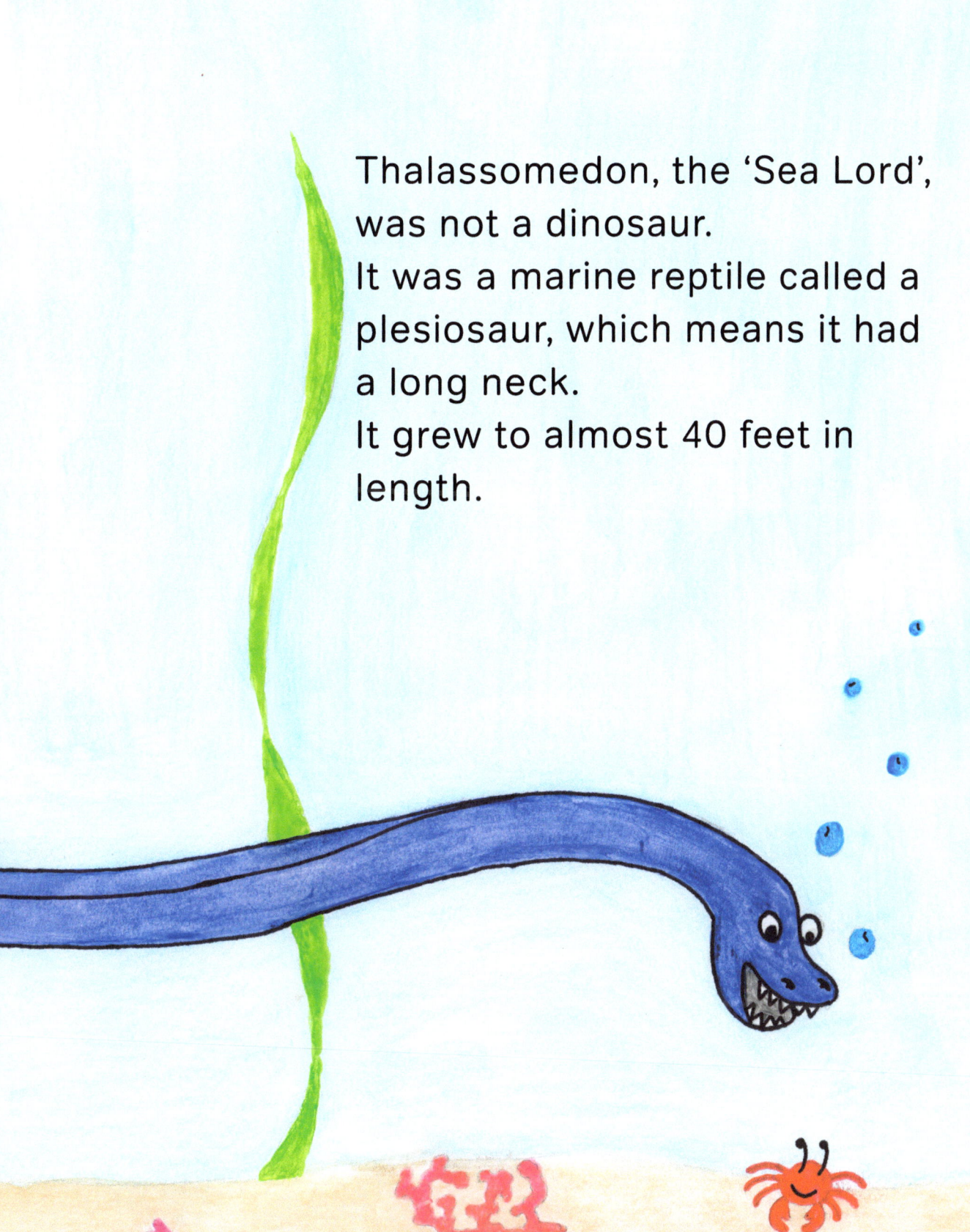

Thalassomedon, the 'Sea Lord', was not a dinosaur.
It was a marine reptile called a plesiosaur, which means it had a long neck.
It grew to almost 40 feet in length.

Liopleurodon was a marine reptile called a pliosaur, which means it had a short neck.
Its name means 'smooth-sided tooth' because one side of its 4-inch-long teeth was smooth.

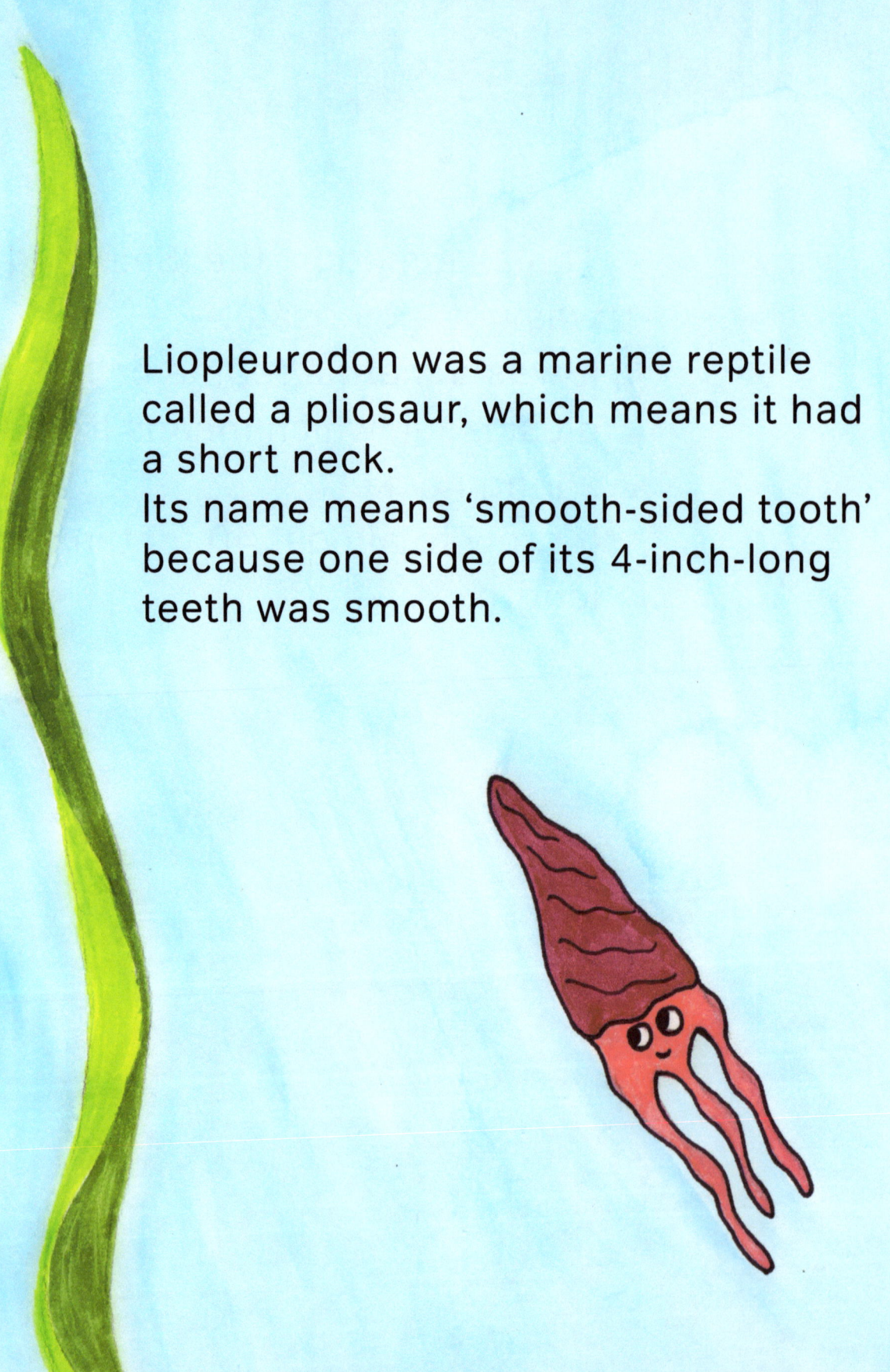

Pteranodon was a flying reptile called a pterosaur.
It had a large crest and would fly over oceans looking for fish to eat.

Triceratops means 'Three Horned Face'.
Two of its horns were as long as three feet.
They used the horns to protect themselves from predators.
They were considered herbivores and ate low growing plants.

Stegosaurus means 'Roofed Lizard' named after the 17 plates on its back.
It also had spikes on its tail for protection from predators.
It was an herbivore that ate mostly leaves and ferns.

Tyrannosaurus Rex was the most famous dinosaur of all.
The 'Tyrant Lizard King' was 15 feet tall and had 58 teeth, the largest being 6 inches long. Even though he had small arms he was one of the most powerful carnivores on land.

Glossary

Carnivore: an animal that eats meat

Herbivore: an animal that eats only plants

Omnivore: an animal that eats both meat and plants

Plesiosaur: A marine reptile with four flippers. Many had very long necks.

Pliosaur: A type of plesiosaur, with a shorter neck, larger head and jaws.

Pterosaur: An ancient flying reptile with skin covered wings.

Drawn by Damien age 7

Pronunciation

Spinosaurus: SPIEN-oh-SOR-us

Brachiosaurus: BRAK-ee-oh-SOR-us

Ornithomimus: or-NITH-o-MIEM-us

Thalassomedon: tha-LAS-o-MEE-don

Liopleurodon: LIE-oh-PLOOR-oh-don

Plesiosaur: PLEE-see-uh-sor

Pliosaur: PLY-uh-sor

Pterosaur: TER-o-SAWR

Pteranodon: ter-AN-oh-don

Triceratops: tri-SEH-ruh-tops

Stegosaurus: STEG-o-SOR-us

Tyrannosaurus Rex: ti-RAN-o-SOR-us